Puppet Pals

Written by
Annie Temple

Photographs by
John Paul Endress

Celebration Press
Parsippany, New Jersey

Meet my puppets!
One is a bear.

One is a dog.

One is a zebra.

One is a frog.

One is a seal.

The seal has a ball!

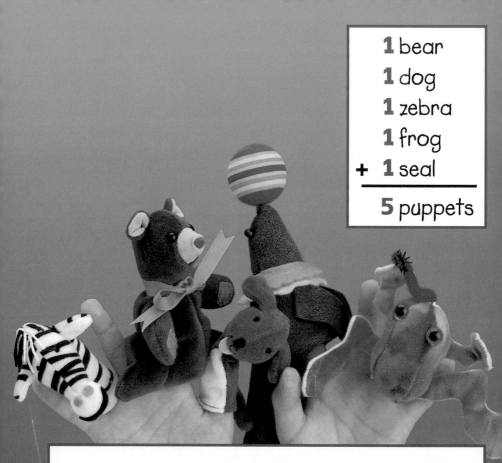

1 bear
1 dog
1 zebra
1 frog
+ 1 seal
─────
5 puppets

How many puppets are there in all?